The Deep Knowledge Y

The Gift of Not Belonging Workbook Edition

Written by Dr. Anika Rehn, Psy.D.

📓 COPYRIGHT PAGE

Essential Concepts and Action Steps
from *The Gift of Not Belonging* Workbook Edition
© 2025 by Dr. Anika Rehn, Psy.D.
All rights reserved. No part of this publication may be reproduced, stored in a
retrieval system, or transmitted in any form by any means—electronic,
mechanical, photocopying, recording, or otherwise—without prior written
permission of the publisher.

Published by Greywave Publishing
Printed in the United States of America
First Edition, July 2025

Cover design by Greywave Studio
Interior design by Precision Typesetters

For permissions, inquiries, or bulk orders, contact:
Greywave Publishing
3424 Sanderlin Avenue
Portland, Oregon, USA

✎ FOREWORD

This is not a workbook for the crowd-pleasers.

This is a workbook for those who always felt a little off-center in the room—for those who could walk into a gathering, be greeted with smiles, and still feel unseen.

The world rewards joiners. It hands out approval in bulk. It praises team players and group thinkers. But what happens when you're wired for solitude, autonomy, and depth? What happens when the places where others find meaning just feel like noise to you?

The *Gift of Not Belonging* isn't about rebellion. It's about *reorientation*. This workbook is a place to unearth your personal mechanics—your otrovert nature—and finally stop apologizing for it.

It's not self-help. It's self-reclamation.

These pages won't nudge you toward social skills or try to fix your relationship with the group. Instead, they'll arm you with tools to clarify your own voice, locate your true rhythm, and live outside the herd—without shame, without performance, and without compromise.

Do the work. Don't belong. And thrive anyway.

—Dr. Anika Rehn

TABLE OF CONTENTS

CHAPTER 1: What Is an Otrovert?... 6

CHAPTER 2: How the World Misunderstands Otroverts........... 16

CHAPTER 3: The Meek Rebel... 25

CHAPTER 4: The Pseudo Extrovert... 34

CHAPTER 5: The Creative... 43

CHAPTER 6: The Empath... 52

CHAPTER 7: We Are All Born Otroverts....................................... 61

CHAPTER 8: A Culture That Rewards Joining............................ 70

CHAPTER 9: The Fallacy of Fitting In... 79

CHAPTER 1: What Is an Otrovert?

• Chapter Objectives

- To define and differentiate the concept of *otroversion* from introversion and extroversion

- To dismantle false assumptions that make otroverts feel broken or socially deficient

- To initiate a shift from pathologizing disconnection to honoring deep individuality

• Teaching: Otroversion Is Not a Flaw—It's a Frequency

Most people navigate life on either end of the introvert-extrovert binary. But you? You've been on a different bandwidth your whole life—misread, mislabeled, and misunderstood.

You weren't quiet—you just didn't need to dominate the air.
You weren't antisocial—you just didn't like the script.
You weren't rebellious—you just didn't join.

Otroversion is not a syndrome. It's a signal. It's the *true north* of a person who *functions best outside the group structure.* You're not afraid of people. You're not drained by intimacy. But what you crave is **depth without dilution**—connection without conformity.

And in a society obsessed with collective belonging, being otroverted often feels like a social error code. But this workbook is your diagnostic override. Being an otrovert is not an absence of something—it's a *presence of something else.* A self-guided orientation. A different way of hearing the music.

This chapter invites you to *fucking stop explaining yourself.* You're not built to fit in. You're built to tune in—to your own signal. The first task is to name that signal. Claim it. And stop trying to convert it.

◆ Key Lessons

- **Otroversion is not social anxiety.** It's a deep preference for self-sourced belonging rather than group-sourced identity.

- **Your disinterest in group rituals doesn't make you cold—it means you require authenticity to engage.** You don't play by false social contracts. That's not dysfunction. That's integrity.

- **You likely attract others but repel crowds.** Your presence can be magnetic one-on-one, but disorienting in collectives. That's not a contradiction—it's your signature frequency.

- **You've likely spent a lifetime self-abandoning to meet others' comfort levels.** This workbook will end that habit. Permanently.

- **Otroversion is a form of relational sovereignty.** You don't belong *to* groups. You choose *when* and *how* to connect—without being devoured by it.

◆ Self-Reflection Prompts

1. When did you first notice that you didn't enjoy groups the way others seemed to?

2. Have you ever been praised for being outgoing, but still felt unseen? Describe that contradiction.

3. Where in your life do you still fake "group enthusiasm"? Why do you maintain that performance?

4. What specific social patterns feel the most foreign or performative to you?

5. What behaviors have others misinterpreted as aloof, arrogant, or antisocial—when they were actually just you protecting your energy?

6. How do you show warmth or connection without using the typical group dynamics?

7. What part of your otroversion do you feel most ashamed of—aŋd why?

8. Do you feel relief when plaŋs get canceled? Be hoŋest—what's behiŋd that?

9. In what moments do you feel most fully yourself—socially or otherwise?

10. What's one social habit you're ready to retire forever?

_____

_____

◆ Action Prompts

- **Write a one-page Manifesto of Otroversion.** No apologies, no soft language. Declare how you move through the world and what you reject. Post it somewhere only you see.

- **Stop attending one event this month that drains your energy.** Don't explain your absence. Don't compensate with guilt. Just let your no be clean.

- **Replace a default group habit with a solo ritual.** If you usually do weekly brunches, try a solo creative session instead. Watch how it feeds you differently.

- **Tell one person the truth about how you feel in groups.** Choose someone who doesn't demand belonging from you, and speak from clarity—not apology.

- **Start tracking your *thriving conditions*.** Make a list of social setups that *energize* you vs. *drain* you. Rebuild your life around the first list. Burn the second.

CHAPTER 2: How the World Misunderstands Otroverts

◆ Chapter Objectives

- To reveal how society constantly misdiagnoses otroversion as a flaw

- To separate social expectation from actual psychological need

- To begin reclaiming personal truth from public misunderstanding

◆ Teaching: The Culture of Mislabeling

The world doesn't know what to do with someone who doesn't want to *join* it. So it starts calling them names: antisocial, cold, "different," distant, avoidant, arrogant.

Otroverts have been shoved into wrong categories their entire lives—told they're shy when they're discerning, told they're rebellious when they're simply autonomous, told they're awkward when they're just uninterested in performing.

Mass misunderstanding isn't a reflection of your failure to conform—it's *proof that the framework is broken.* The crowd doesn't have better answers. It just has more volume.

This chapter isn't about winning anyone over. It's about burning the damn scorecard.

You don't need to explain yourself to a world that's designed to misunderstand you. You need to *unhook from the need to be interpreted accurately.*

You were never meant to be read by the masses. You were meant to be understood by the few, and *seen by yourself.*

- **Key Lessons**

  - **Otroverts are often miscast as introverts or extroverts because their rhythm doesn't match the binary.** The failure isn't yours—it's the lens.

  - **Society rewards visibility, not authenticity.** When you pull back from the spotlight, people assume you're broken, not strategic.

  - **Most social systems are built around compliance—not connection.** If you don't comply, you're seen as the problem. That's the setup.

  - **You've been trained to mask your true social needs in exchange for surface acceptance.** Undoing that programming will make people uncomfortable—and that's okay.

  - **Misunderstanding is inevitable when the culture is built for joiners.** Your clarity is not for them—it's for you.

◆ Self-Reflection Prompts

1. When have you felt most misunderstood socially?

2. What label have people put on you that never felt true?

3. Have you ever tried to explain your nature and felt dismissed or patronized?

_____

_____

_____

_____

_____

_____

_____

4. What traits in you make others uncomfortable—but are actually your strengths?

_____

_____

_____

_____

_____

5. When have you silenced your real social preferences just to keep the peace?

6. How often do you let yourself move *at your own pace* in social situations?

7. What's the most insulting thing someone's assumed about your personality?

8. What part of yourself do you still feel the need to justify to others?

9. Who *actually* understands you—and why do you think they do?

10. Are you still waiting to be fully "seen"? What would it take for that to stop mattering?

◆ Action Prompts

- **Burn the labels.** Write down every inaccurate label you've carried—then destroy the list. Rip it. Burn it. Bury it. Get fucking rid of it.

- **Craft a new language.** Redefine three of your most misunderstood traits using *your* vocabulary. Don't use psychological jargon—use *truthful power*.

- **Say no without a reason.** Pick one social ask this week and decline without justification. No explanation. No guilt. Just sovereignty.

- **Call out the misunderstanding (quietly).** In your journal, write out the ways people misread you. Then write what's actually happening internally. Contrast them. Own both.

- **Exit a social script.** Quit one performative routine—whether it's fake smiles at work or pretending to enjoy "small talk" at family events. Exit. Cold.

CHAPTER 3: The Meek Rebel

◆ Chapter Objectives

- To expose the quiet resistance that defines many otroverts beneath their surface calm

- To differentiate rebellion born from ego versus rebellion rooted in self-preservation

- To cultivate pride in subtle defiance rather than shame for not conforming

---

◆ Teaching: Not Loud, but Unshakeable

You don't wave banners. You don't flip tables. But make no mistake—you are a *rebel*. A fucking surgical one.

The world expects rebellion to be loud, dramatic, explosive. But for the otrovert, rebellion often looks like **silence in the face of absurdity**. It looks like walking away when everyone else claps. It looks like refusing to fake-laugh at power. It looks like opting out *without making a scene*.

That's your genius. You dismantle systems by not needing them. You don't fight for a seat at the table—you walk away and build your own goddamn room.

You've likely been called "too sensitive," "too serious," "too much," or even "not enough." But all along, you were living on your own frequency, rejecting what didn't align.

This chapter will help you see your quiet refusal not as failure to engage, but as **strategic disengagement**. Your rebellion is not in volume—it's in refusal. And refusal is a fucking power move.

◆ Key Lessons

- **Meek rebellion is rooted in clarity, not cowardice.** It's the act of saying "no" without performing resistance for applause.

- **Otroverts often withdraw not to avoid conflict, but to starve false systems of their energy.** That's power disguised as absence.

- **Society conditions us to equate silence with surrender.** But your silence is often loaded with defiance—one they can't control.

- **You've probably been punished for noncompliance even when you didn't protest.** That's because your refusal threatens group validation.

- **You don't need to be seen resisting for your resistance to matter.** Subtle defiance creates fractures in expectation—and that's where real change starts.

◆ Self-Reflection Prompts

1. When have you silently refused something everyone around you accepted?

2. Have you ever been labeled passive when you were actually being deliberate?

3. What social "norm" do you quietly reject, even if you still participate in it?

4. In what ways have you preserved your own integrity through strategic silence?

5. When did you last *not explain* yourself—and it felt fucking right?

6. What parts of you revolt even when your mouth stays shut?

7. What's your relationship with the word "meek"? What feelings does it stir up?

8. Where do you still wish you had rebelled more clearly in the past?

9. Who in your life fears your quiet distance? What does that say about them?

10. How could you start honoring your resistance as a form of intelligence instead of shame?

◆ Action Prompts

- **Write a Rebellion Inventory.** List every time you walked away, stayed silent, or opted out *on purpose.* Not to avoid—but to preserve. Honor every one.

- **Refuse once this week—with zero explanation.** It could be a request, a norm, a comment. Say "No." That's it.

- **Identify a social contract you never signed—but are still performing.** Break it. Opt out. Stop playing.

- **Reread one "meek" moment from your past—and reframe it as courageous.** Journal what strength it actually took.

- **Speak it once.** Choose one rebellion you've never admitted to anyone—and say it out loud to someone who has earned your honesty.

CHAPTER 4: The Pseudo Extrovert

◆ Chapter Objectives

- To unmask the performance of extroversion used for survival, success, or acceptance

- To explore the emotional and energetic toll of living as a pseudo-extrovert

- To begin shedding the false persona and reclaim authentic rhythm

◆ Teaching: The Mask You Mastered

You know how to perform. Hell, you probably *excel* at it.

You've smiled when you wanted to leave. You've entertained when you needed stillness. You've played "fun" when all you wanted was fucking depth.

This is the chapter where we rip off the mask.

Pseudo-extroverts are otroverts who've become fluent in the social language—but every word is a translation. You've learned the jokes, the postures, the rhythms. And no one suspects how much you're *not okay* during the applause.

You've tricked them. But more dangerously, you may have tricked *yourself.* The applause feels like approval. The parties feel like "being normal." The team celebrations feel like success. But the next morning you feel **hollow as fuck**.

Your mastery of extroversion kept you safe. But now it's *killing your clarity.* This chapter is about ending the performance and returning to your **inner language**.

- **Key Lessons**

  - **Pseudo-extroversion is a learned mask—polished to survive, but never meant to be permanent.** It's fluent, but it's not fluent in *you*.

  - **Your ability to engage doesn't mean you thrive in it.** You can host, joke, lead—and still feel utterly misaligned.

  - **The praise you get for being "so outgoing" can be the most dangerous poison.** It teaches you to betray your own rhythm for external validation.

  - **You're not broken for being good at things that exhaust you.** You're just out of sync with your real architecture.

  - **Letting the mask drop may mean disappointing people—but it'll finally *nourish you*.**

◆ Self-Reflection Prompts

1. What aspects of extroversion have you mastered, even if they drain you?

2. What does it cost you—mentally, emotionally, physically—to maintain that image?

3. When did you first realize you were faking parts of your "outgoing" self?

_____

_____

_____

_____

_____

_____

_____

4. What fear keeps you from dropping the extrovert performance?

_____

_____

_____

_____

_____

_____

_____

5. What would your ideal day look like if you weren't performing for anyone?

6. What social compliments make you feel empty inside?

7. Who benefits the most from your pseudo-extroversion? And who are you protecting?

8. When was the last time you disappointed someone by showing your real social needs?

9. What does your body feel like when you're performing extroversion? Describe it in physical terms.

10. What mask are you ready to bury for good?

◆ Action Prompts

- **Choose not to lead.** In a group setting this week, resist the urge to be the host, the energizer, the bridge. Sit back. Watch what happens.

- **Confess the mask.** Tell one person—someone you trust—that your "outgoing self" isn't the whole story. Let them meet the quiet you.

- **Cancel one social obligation you would've faked your way through.** Don't go. Let absence do its work.

- **Practice saying, "I'm not up for that right now."** No apology. No false excuse. Just *truth*.

- **Write your exit plan.** Detail how you'll begin phasing out the extrovert persona from one part of your life. Be brutal. Be honest. Be free.

CHAPTER 5: The Creative

◆ Chapter Objectives

- To link otroversion with the deeper architecture of creativity

- To dismantle the myth that creativity needs crowds or constant feedback

- To harness solitude as a sacred wellspring of original thought and emotional refinement

◆ Teaching: Creativity Without an Audience

Otroverts often carry a potent creative charge—but it's not *for show*. It doesn't seek applause. It doesn't ask for permission. It's not some glittery expression tied to external validation. It's a *fucking lifeline*.

Your creativity doesn't come alive in brainstorming circles or team synergy. It comes alive when the world finally shuts the hell up—when you're alone with the raw, electric pulse of your own thoughts.

This chapter strips away the noise that tells you creativity needs community, collaboration, or a cheering crowd. It reclaims the creative life as a *solitary ritual,* not a performance.

You don't create to be liked. You create to survive.

Otroverts make art, systems, visions, music, movements—not because they want to join the scene, but because they want to *transcend it.* Your imagination is your home. It is your identity. It is your rebellion.

Honor it. Protect it. And stop fucking apologizing for not wanting to share it with everyone.

◆ Key Lessons

- Otroverts are often creative not because they crave expression—but because creativity is their **language of** *existence*. It's not elective—it's instinctual.

- **You don't need creative "accountability partners."** You need silence, time, and the right to vanish into your own flow.

- **Collaboration can feel like dilution.** If the group poisons the well, drink alone.

- **You've probably been told your ideas are "too much," "too weird," or "too intense." That's code for: they weren't ready.** Keep going anyway.

- **You're not a struggling artist—you're a** *sovereign* *one*. **Your isolation isn't a failure. It's a forge.**

◆ Self-Reflection Prompts

1. What creative urges have you suppressed to be more "socially acceptable"?

———————————————————————
———————————————————————
———————————————————————
———————————————————————
———————————————————————
———————————————————————
———————————————————————

2. When do your ideas feel most alive—and who is *never* in the room when that happens?

———————————————————————
———————————————————————
———————————————————————
———————————————————————
———————————————————————
———————————————————————
———————————————————————

3. How many times have you dumbed down your vision for easier digestion by others?

4. Where do you create from: revenge, longing, truth, pain, defiance—or all of the above?

5. What part of your creative self still feels misunderstood or unseen?

_____

_____

_____

_____

_____

_____

6. Who tries to *cheerlead* your creativity but clearly doesn't get it?

_____

_____

_____

_____

_____

_____

_____

7. What ideas have you quietly protected out of fear they'd be mocked or misused?

8. If no one could ever see your work again, would you still make it? Why?

9. What rhythms or environments feed your best creative work?

10. What's your creative "home"—the place in your soul that never tries to impress, only to reveal?

◆ Action Prompts

- **Create something this week that no one will see.** Don't photograph it. Don't share it. Make it, love it, and let it live in secret.

- **Audit your creative routines.** Highlight which ones feel performative vs. nourishing. Cut one performance. Replace it with ritual.

- **Write a Creative Oath.** Declare who you make for (yourself), why you create (to survive), and what you will no longer compromise (your soul).

- **Burn the committee.** Mentally fire the "audience in your head" that edits your work. Write their names. Cross them out. Create without them.

- **Build your studio, not your stage.** Reorganize one room or corner to reflect your private vision. Let it become sacred, not social.

CHAPTER 6: The Empath

◆ Chapter Objectives

- To explore how otroverts often carry heightened emotional sensitivity

- To uncover how overstimulation and emotional absorption lead to social exhaustion

- To build internal boundaries that preserve emotional clarity and sovereignty

---

◆ Teaching: The Emotional Absorber in a Loud World

Otroverts are often empaths. Not because they choose to be—but because their system *doesn't have a filter*. You don't just *notice* energy—you *absorb* it. You don't hear people—you *feel* them, sometimes *before* they speak.

This sensitivity isn't weakness—it's a high-voltage radar. But when surrounded by noise, expectations, or inauthentic people, that radar becomes a **fucking curse**. You don't just leave drained—you leave *fragmented*.

Being an empathic otrovert means you often feel too much, too fast, too deep. And society doesn't give you time to process—it just tells you to "get over it" or "stop being dramatic."

This chapter is about learning the difference between *caring* and *carrying*. You're not the emotional landfill of the world. You are not required to feel everything just because you can.

Your empathy is sacred. But it's not *free*. It needs rules. It needs rest. It needs **fierce boundaries**. Or it will destroy you.

- **Key Lessons**

  - **Empathy without boundaries is emotional slavery.** You're not weak—you're wide open. That's dangerous without control.

  - **Otroverts are often emotional mirrors.** People unconsciously dump their mess into your nervous system. You reflect it—but it's not yours.

  - **Being sensitive doesn't mean being responsible for everyone else's comfort.** Your job is to *feel truth*, not to fix feelings.

  - **You need solitude not just to recharge, but to *cleanse*.** Social overstimulation isn't tiring—it's contaminating.

  - **Real empathy is selective.** If you give it to everyone, you lose yourself. And then there's nothing left to feel *with*.

◆ Self-Reflection Prompts

1. Who are the people that emotionally exhaust you the fastest? Why?

2. When have you taken on someone else's emotional weight and it made you physically sick or mentally spiraled?

3. What emotions do you habitually absorb from others without realizing it?

_____

4. Have you ever felt guilty for not wanting to "help" someone emotionally?

_____

5. How do you protect your emotional space before or after socializing?

6. When did someone mistake your silence for agreement—but you were just feeling everything at once?

7. What's your earliest memory of being overwhelmed by another person's emotion?

8. How do you decompress after absorbing too much emotion in one day?

9. What rituals, objects, or spaces help you return to yourself?

10. If you believed your empathy was sacred, how would you treat it differently?

◆ Action Prompts

- **Start filtering.** Before any interaction, ask yourself: "Do I want to *feel this person* right now?" If not, shield. Withdraw. Protect.

- **Install recovery time.** After every emotionally intense situation, give yourself *non-negotiable decompression space.* Silence is medicine.

- **Return what's not yours.** After feeling overloaded, speak aloud: "This is not mine." Visualize it leaving your body. Repeat until light.

- **Design a cleansing ritual.** Create a weekly or nightly practice to purge absorbed emotion—through movement, water, breath, or fire.

- **Speak one boundary aloud.** Tell someone close to you, "I can't absorb that right now." Practice not rescuing.

CHAPTER 7: We Are All Born Otroverts

◆ Chapter Objectives

- To challenge the myth that belonging is a natural human default

- To reframe otroversion as an original state, not an anomaly

- To explore how cultural conditioning suppresses independent identity from birth

◆ Teaching: The Original Self Was Sovereign

You weren't born to belong. You were born **whole**.

Before the school assemblies.
Before the team sports.
Before the cliques and clubs.
Before the identity labels and personality types.

You existed—quietly, curiously, instinctively—in your own space. And it was fucking *enough*. You didn't need a tribe to validate your breath. You didn't require consensus to form your thoughts. You didn't look for crowds—you looked for **clarity**.

This chapter isn't about becoming an otrovert. It's about **remembering** that you were one *before they trained it out of you.*

The group came later. The performance came later. The longing for approval? Injected.

You were born with boundaries. With rhythm. With truth.

Otroversion isn't rare. It's just been smothered. If the culture hadn't conditioned it out of you, you'd still be living in it.

This chapter is your *origin story reclamation*. You don't owe anyone a return to the herd. You owe yourself a return to your *unbent self*.

◆ Key Lessons

- **Otroversion is not a deviation—it's the original setting before cultural programming kicked in.** You are returning, not transforming.

- **The human need for connection has been confused with the craving for conformity.** The first is real. The second is trained.

- **We are born attuned to internal cues—not group consensus.** Otroverts simply stayed loyal to those cues longer.

- **Children who don't join are often labeled as "shy," "weird," or "antisocial"—but they're usually just uncolonized.** That was you.

- **This world doesn't need more joiners—it needs more original rhythms.** And you're the blueprint.

◆ Self-Reflection Prompts

1. What aspects of your childhood show signs of original otroversion?

---

2. When did you first start faking enthusiasm for group activities?

---

3. What "good child" behavior was really just early masking of your true rhythm?

4. Who first told you that fitting in was a requirement? What did they gain from that?

5. What games, environments, or rituals did you *hate* but never said so?

6. If you could speak to your child-self, what would you tell them about the power of not belonging?

7. What memories of solitude felt holy or vivid as a child?

8. How did you cope when others tried to force you into group identity?

9. What part of your original self still lives inside you, untouched?

10. What would you reclaim if you believed otroversion was your birthright?

◆ Action Prompts

- **Write to your child-self.** One page. No platitudes. Just truth: "Here's who you were. Here's what they tried to erase. Here's what I'm reclaiming."

- **Re-enact a solo ritual from childhood.** It could be drawing alone, taking long walks, playing pretend in silence—do it now, as an act of reclamation.

- **Untrain a belief.** Identify one message you internalized about "needing to belong." Write it out, then destroy it. Replace it with one truth.

- **Create a Belonging Filter.** For every new invite, ask: "Is this connection or compliance?" Only say yes to the first.

- **Post a visible reminder.** Somewhere in your space, place a phrase that reminds you: *"I was born whole. I don't need to join to exist."*

CHAPTER 8: A Culture That Rewards Joining

- **Chapter Objectives**

  - To expose the hidden architecture of groupism embedded in society

  - To reveal how collective conformity is sold as morality, progress, or productivity

  - To begin mentally exiting the performance economy of group-based validation

- **Teaching: The Worship of the Crowd**

This world doesn't reward truth. It rewards participation.
Doesn't reward clarity. It rewards *compliance*.
Doesn't reward sovereignty. It rewards *spectacle*.

From kindergarten to corporate, everything's wired to make you **join**: clubs, teams, causes, performances, groupthink, groupfeel, group-fucking-everything.

The "team player" gets the promotion. The loud one gets the mic. The compliant one gets the praise. Meanwhile, the otrovert—who actually sees what's broken—gets benched for not pretending to be thrilled about it.

This isn't accidental. It's structural.

The culture doesn't want self-defined people. It wants performers. It wants unity at the cost of *truth*. It wants harmony at the cost of *clarity*. It wants joiners.

But joining, for you, costs too much. It costs your nervous system. Your voice. Your time. Your *fucking soul*.

This chapter is not just about noticing the system—it's about **opting out** of the reward loop. What the culture celebrates is irrelevant if it starves you.

◆ Key Lessons

- **Group identity is rewarded because it's easier to control.** The lone mind is a threat. That's why they keep calling it "antisocial."

- **Belonging is often a bribe.** You get love, as long as you behave.

- **Otroverts threaten systems because they can't be flattered into silence.** That's not a bug. That's the whole fucking point.

- **Every institution pushes joining as virtue—school, religion, politics, even social media.** Non-joiners are shamed, not studied.

- **The cost of belonging is often invisibility.** You're *there*—but not *you*. Otroverts refuse to pay that toll.

◆ Self-Reflection Prompts

1. Where in your life are you still joiŋing out of habit—not desire?

2. What rewards have you received for preteŋding to be a joiŋer? Did they actually nourish you?

3. When have you been punished—subtly or openly—for choosing not to participate?

4. What systems have you felt most alien in, even if you never said so?

5. What "inclusive" environments actually made you feel more isolated or fake?

6. What's the worst thing that would happen if you stopped joining altogether?

7. How have your gifts been overlooked or misread because you didn't "play the game"?

8. What spaces make you feel truly free to be unjoiŋed, unmasked, unmoŋitored?

9. When did you last watch a group dynamic and think, "This is insane"?

10. What rewards are you finally ready to stop chasing?

◆ Action Prompts

- **Audit the rewards.** Make a list of all the "trophies" you've collected for performing group norms. Rank them by hollowness. Burn the top three.

- **Reject one group identity this week.** Say no to something performative—publicly or privately. You don't owe the group a show.

- **Create a No-Praise Policy.** Any time someone praises you for being agreeable or energetic in groups, respond with: "I'm actually happiest alone." Let them feel it.

- **Design your unjoining ritual.** A symbolic act or phrase you use to mentally exit the performance economy. Use it daily.

- **Confront the fear of exile.** Write down what you believe will happen if you stop playing along. Then write the truth: *"I still exist without them."*

CHAPTER 9: The Fallacy of Fitting In

◆ Chapter Objectives

- To dismantle the myth that fitting in is the path to peace, worth, or identity

- To explore the emotional cost of assimilation and the trauma of belonging through self-erasure

- To anchor the reader in radical internal self-belonging—no group required

◆ Teaching: Belonging Is Not the Prize

Let's end the lie.

Fitting in is not safety. It's not success. It's not salvation. It's a slow fucking death—of instinct, identity, and inner alignment.

You've tried to contort. You've tried to comply. You've smiled through teeth-grinding dinners and nodded through conversations that scraped your soul. And for what? For a seat at a table that *feeds everyone but you?*

Otroverts know this: **belonging that costs you your self isn't belonging. It's a hostage deal.**

This final chapter is a kill-switch for that delusion. Fitting in is a cage, not a cure.

Stop trying to make the room love you. Stop filtering yourself to keep peace. Stop shrinking to avoid discomfort. If a space demands you amputate your depth, your rhythm, your solitude—it is not your fucking space.

The fallacy isn't just that you should belong. The fallacy is that belonging is even worth the price they ask.

You don't need to belong. You need to be **anchored inside yourself** so deeply that no exile shakes you.

This is where your power begins: when you stop asking, *"Where do I fit?"* and start declaring, *"I exist. And I'm not going anywhere."*

◆ Key Lessons

- **Fitting in often means *flattening* your edges.** Your real self has sharpness. Depth. Complexity. That's not a flaw—it's your form.

- **Belonging that requires masking is a form of quiet violence.** If they only accept the version of you that performs, you are not accepted.

- **Otroverts carry a selfhood so intact that groups often find it threatening.** That doesn't mean shrink—it means *stand firmer*.

- **You've been conditioned to treat exile like failure.** But exile is often the first sign of awakening.

- **Internal belonging trumps external applause every time.** You are not lonely—you are finally *alone enough to hear your own voice*.

◆ Self-Reflection Prompts

1. What parts of yourself have you hidden or silenced just to fit in?

2. What emotions do you feel when you're "included" but still unseen?

3. What groups or roles have you outgrown but still cling to out of fear?

4. Have you ever betrayed your own boundaries for the illusion of connection?

5. What group behaviors have you mimicked just to survive the moment?

6. What version of you would emerge if you stopped giving a damn about fitting in?

7. When was the last time you felt at home in yourself—even in exile from others?

_____

_____

_____

_____

_____

_____

_____

8. Who do you become when you're finally alone, unobserved, and free?

_____

_____

_____

_____

_____

_____

_____

9. What would "internal belonging" look like in your daily life?

10. What's one phrase that could become your personal mantra of sovereign selfhood?

◆ Action Prompts

- **Break the fitting-in addiction.** List every group or circle where you currently shrink. One by one, write a sentence reclaiming your space—or your exit.

- **Design your Belonging Contract.** Write terms for what *real* belonging means to you. If a space can't meet those terms—it's not a match.

- **Practice visible non-compliance.** In one public setting, show up as fully you—unmasked, unapologetic. Let them react. Let it roll off.

- **Initiate a Self-Witnessing Ritual.** Every day, acknowledge one act where you honored your truth instead of conforming. Record it. Build a track record.

- **Celebrate the exile.** Write an Ode to Not Fitting In. Make it fierce. Frame it. Let it replace your need for applause.

Printed in Dunstable, United Kingdom